EDUCATING OUR GIRLS

A Way Forward

The Right to Education is a Basic Human Right.
— Dr. Ejiro U. Osiobe

Ejiro U. Osiobe

Educating Our Girls
© 2024 Ejiro U. Osiobe
© 2021 Ane Osiobe International Foundation.

Paperback: ISBN: 978-1-64318-132-5
Hardback: ISBN: 978-1-64318-133-2
Ebook: ISBN: 978-1-64318-135-6

IMPERIUM PUBLISHING

1097 N 400 Rd
Baldwin City, KS, 66006
www.imperiumpublishing.com

EDUCATING OUR GIRLS

A Way Forward

Ejiro U. Osiobe

Baker University Assistant Professor
Founder of The Ane Osiobe International Foundation

IMPERIUM PUBLISHING
CREATE YOUR STORY

Investing in a nation's Educational System will inevitably move that country's Production-Possibility Frontier outward.

— Dr. Ejiro U. Osiobe

Preface

The roles, rights, and privileges of (fe)males have been controversial for decades. Most societies around the globe are faced with balancing these rights as we navigate through time. This book examines the importance of female education and mentions notable women who have done exploits.

Contents

Preface

The author(s) hereby declare that generative AI technologies, such as image-producing models, have been used in the image generation of this manuscript. This explanation includes the name, version, model, and source of the generative AI technology, as well as all input prompts provided to it.

Details of the AI usage are given below:

1. OpenArt SDXL: image prompts – African schools, school girls, African school children, Nigerian classroom
2. Picsart Free Image Generator: image prompts – Nigeran schools, school girls, African school children, Nigerian classroom

INTRODUCTION

Productivity, innovation, investment, and trade are essential to any economy's growth, and education ensures the quality of its progress. Female education must be encouraged in Nigeria to foster social development, particularly if the growth dividend is

Investing in Special Needs Children in the city of Abuja, Nigeria
© Ane Osiobe International Foundation

not shared equitably and the wage gap by choice of profession is to be leveled. Although the economic and social cost of the great lockdown hasn't yet been identified as cities are still partially or fully closed, the crisis continues to weigh heavily on Nigerians, with unemployment increasing and relative poverty affecting millions more. In Nigeria, the gap between the richest and the poorest is widening, youth unemployment remains high, and access to social services remains elusive for many. Today, Nigerians' are looking for ways to spur economic

Supplying a high school with back-to-school materials in Abuja © Ane Osiobe International Foundation

growth in their local communities, hence the Ane Osiobe International Foundation promoting education in the continent. The foundation's contributions to this effort include but are not limited to supplying children with back-to-school materials, books, and uniforms, paying for standards exams, writing academic papers, technical reports, and books, and supplying residential schools with food by creating a farm. This book highlights women's achievements worldwide, especially in Nigeria, while providing ample evidence of the critical role all the great women played with their education and skills in fostering social progress. Over the past decades, we have witnessed an increase in the awareness of the importance of female education. The right of female children to quality education has led to the evaluation of girls' schooling in society. Many governmental and non-governmental agencies have raised voices, initiated programs, and delegated funds to the educational transformation of girls worldwide. With all the efforts put in place, we seek to look deeply at the present state of things as regards:

- The level of improvement made and the new challenges emerging as a result.
- How effective have the orders, rights, and campaigns been?
- Are female children receiving the attention needed to succeed in the education environment?

Educating women has been identified as a backbone of advanced societies worldwide [1]. It is an important issue for several reasons: female education significantly reduces the rate of maternal mortality in communities [1] [2] [3]; this is so because women who undergo formal training (formal, informal, and cultural), knowledge, labor, skills (general, industry, firm, job, and task-specific); experience [4] tend to have a better understanding of healthcare.

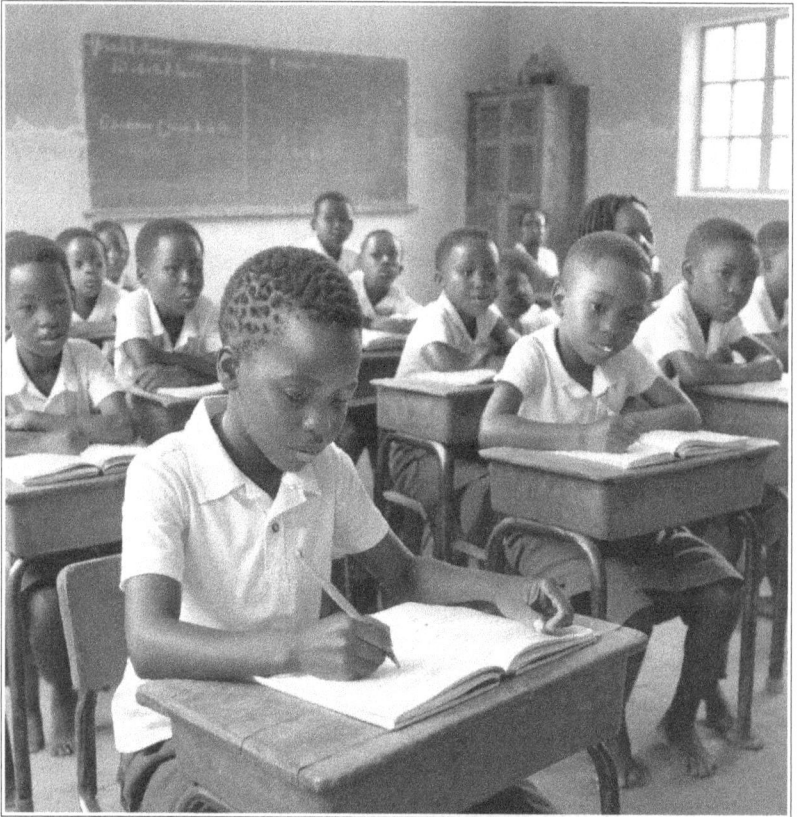

Educating boys has always been a priority in most cultures.
(Image created in OpenArt)

In the 21st century, education is one of the most critical areas of empowerment for young adults; it also offers some of the most sustainable solutions to the issues we face today.

Offering girls' education is one sure way to prepare them for the challenges of tomorrow. They can make better choices over the changes they wish to see in their families, communities, and nation. Female education should be encouraged for the sole reason that *"all humans are created equal,"* and the pursuit of happiness and property is a fundamental human right. Education gives women the skills, information, and self-confidence needed for better parenting, work, and citizenship [5]. According to a document released by the [6] on girls' education, it stated that *"Girls' education goes beyond getting a female child into school; it is also about ensuring that these girls learn, contribute, and feel safe while in the school environment."*

Ejiro U. Osiobe

CURRENT CHALLENGES

At first glance, looking at things from the surface, it might seem that all is well *(things are improving, but we can do better)*. Education opportunities are spread evenly between male and female genders in Nigeria. It is certainly not true when you look closer, especially in rural communities.

Nigerian girls with an opportunity to attend school.
(Image created in OpenArt)

15

Despite the existence of unique girls' schools nationwide, more work must be done to encourage more families to send their female children to school. There are many reasons why females in Nigeria are less educated than men. Let us look at the most prominent reasons in precise detail.

Classrooms have traditionally only allowed boys.
(Image created in OpenArt)

Over the years, various researches have proven a connection between girls' literacy rate and religious and traditional misconceptions [7]. Nigeria is a very religious country where most citizens live according to the book of their faith. Their religious beliefs contribute to why many households think that girls don't need formal education as their male counterparts. This same ideology is true in the native traditions of the nation. Most of these traditional views don't believe a girl should do more than become a mother and a homemaker. In such cases, why would parents spend money on giving their female child a formal education when being a mother doesn't need all that? These actions are due to socioeconomic and cultural norms. To tag this as *"**Gender Discrimination**"* will be short-sighted and an assumption that parents don't love their female children, which is not wholly accurate. Today, in very few parts of the world, girls are discriminated against and marginalized *"based on sex"* within their communities and in schools. Many families in Nigeria, especially the ones from the northern part of the nation, suffer from poverty [8]. This prevalent poverty leads parents to prioritize boys' education over that of girls, thereby neglecting girls' education completely or giving it less attention than it deserves [7].

In our society, female achievements are not considered as significant as their male counterpart; this is true because the history of the accomplishments of influential women is usually not taught in our schools [7]. Hence, they do not reflect their contribution to Nigeria and the position(s) they occupy in governmental and non-governmental offices. Thus, the primary reason for writing this book is its primary contribution to women's literature worldwide. Another issue that comes from Nigerian traditional and religious views is a child's early marriage stand. In most cases, female children have little or no say in their decisions. To mitigate this, we recommend educating our children and encouraging them to get a higher-skilled degree at the master's and doctorate levels. When a girl is forced to become a wife at an early age of 11 – 12 years, her right to acquire formal education can be affected, and in most cases, it's for the negative. This is a sensitive and controversial topic, as most girls affected by child marriages do not receive adequate formal education training. To add to this list are the frequent cases of abuse, which might come from both loved ones and strangers [7] [9] [10] [11] [12] [13].

THE BENEFITS
OF EDUCATING WOMEN

Educating girls has a lot of benefits for society and her personal life. We have examined female children's socioeconomic and cultural challenges in acquiring formal education. Now, let us look at the benefits of empowering these girls.

Photo © Ane Osiobe International Foundation

"Educating girls, in any nation, increases the nation's global competitiveness in all sectors of its economy, resulting in improvement and increase in the nation's productivity."

— Ejiro U. Osiobe

According to our founder of the Ane Osiobe International Foundation, educating girls in any nation will lead to a healthy competitive environment, which is necessary for unprecedented economic growth and development. Human capital is one of the pillars of the knowledge-based economy in any educated and skilled labor force. Building on our founder's favorite statement,

"Engagement comes with knowledge, and knowledge comes through education." — Ejiro U. Osiobe.

For innovation, improvement, and development, it becomes necessary to involve both genders. There is no end to the volume of ideas that can emanate from gender equality [14] [15] [16] [17] [18]. Most developed economies of the world found significant contributions due to the active involvement of educated women. Examples:

- **Claudette Colvin**, an African American girl who was expected to give up her seat to a white woman on a bus, refused to get up; she inspired Rosa Parks to do the same nine months later. Many point to it as the first event that started the modern civil rights movement.

    "I knew then, and I know now that when it comes to justice, there is no easy way to get it; you have to take a stand and say this is not right." — Claudette Colvin.

- **Sor Juana Inés de la Cruz** was a 17th-century nun, self-taught scholar, and poem writer. One of her works was the first published argument for a woman's right to Education in America.

  "I don't study to know more, but to ignore less." — Sor Juana Inés de la Cruz.

- **Margaret Chase Smith**, the head of NASA, once noted that we would not have put a man on the moon without the help of Margaret:

  "The right way is not always the popular and easy way; standing for right when it isn't popular is a true test of moral character." — Margaret Chase Smith.

- **Kate Sheppard** traveled around New Zealand and advocated that women deserved voting rights, and in 1893, New Zealand became the first country to give voting rights to EVERY woman in the nation.

  "We must be ourselves at all risk." — Kate Sheppard.

- **Sally Ride** believed young girls could be whatever they want to be when they grow up.

"Young girls need to see role models in whatever careers they choose so that they can picture themselves doing those jobs; you can't be you if you can't see." — Sally Ride.

- **Marie Curie** was the first woman awarded a Nobel prize in physics and chemistry. She was the first person ever to receive two Nobel prizes.

"Nothing in life is to be feared; it is only to be understood." — Marie Curie.

- **Wangari Maathai, Ph.D.**, Green Belt Movement, promoted the planting of trees in Kenya. Her work in protecting the environment and human rights in Kenya made her the first African woman to be awarded a Nobel Peace Prize.

"Today, we are faced with a challenge that calls for a shift in our thinking so that humanity stops threatening its life-support system." — Wangari Maathai.

These women's stories were made known to the world by the beautiful work of Chelsea Clinton and Alexandra Boiger (2017). The economy of nations' experience grows when women are empowered through education because productivity and opportunity are now spread evenly among genders in most parts of the world. If women can generate income at various levels, it reduces dependence and promotes entrepreneurship in the nation. Educating girls reduces inequality, encouraging the idea that we're all created equal. Equality of gender is empowered through literacy among the female members of society. Providing female children the opportunity for formal education makes them relevant to the nation. Opening the primary education system to all *(ensuring they're up to quality standards)* will not just strengthen the female gender group. Still, it will give other marginalized groups, like orphans, ethnic minorities, physically challenged, rural families, and people experiencing poverty, the educational opportunity needed. Because **Emma Lazarus** was right, *"Until we are all free, we are none of us free."*

Back to school at Garki High School
Image © Ane Osiobe International Foundation

Education will empower girls in any society while persuading boys to join their cause and raise their voices against gender violence and oppression of any kind. There are a lot of females who do not know their rights and privileges, and education is the tool for correcting that. As **Nelson Rolihlahla Mandela** said, *"Education is the most powerful weapon you can use to change the world."* While on the other hand, illiteracy has been weaponized over the years to control people. To stop this control, providing access to formal Western education would reduce the rate at which women are abused [8].

Educated young women are healthier and happier community members.
(Image created in Picsart)

Educating all genders in a society is a powerful, lasting solution to poverty. Countries with a low poverty rate have successfully educated the female population, creating a diversified workforce [8] [19] [20] [21] [22]. With all hands on deck, working, and growing the economy, poverty cannot stay in such a community. Equal gender opportunity lowers the rate of infant, child, and maternal mortality [5]. An infant with a learned mother can get better care and safety than an illiterate mother. Literate mothers understand the value of personal hygiene, environmental sanitation, and water purity. A learned

Educated women strengthen their communities.
(Image created in Picsart)

mother easily handles family planning and proper immunization. Because an educated mother knows the importance of adequate nutrition and healthy living, she becomes a significant player in ensuring good health for a long life. A well-educated girl promises a better future for herself, her children, her family, and society [8].

The education of female children will help strengthen democracy in the nation. There is a better chance for women to engage in politics and speak out for the rights of others if they have education as a backbone. With knowledge, women can better serve their nation when they occupy political offices at every level of the government. The skills acquired from their formal education would make the government's decisions more reliable as the women will actively contribute their ideas to trending issues like population control. When women learn their rights, both positive and negative, they are of great value to the world [23].

STEPS TO PROMOTE
FEMALE EDUCATION

According to [24], *"More females go to school and learn to read and write today than in previous decades, and the world, in general, is a much better place."* This means that more

Student giving remarks at a back-to-school event. Lugbe, Nigeria
Image © Ane Osiobe International Foundation

adults will be more likely to be literate in the near future than their parents. A survey that the International Education Statistics in Nigeria did measure literacy across different 5-year age groups. According to the reports, among persons aged 15 to 19 years (those of primary school age in the 1990s), the literacy rate is 70%, but among persons who are 80 years or older, only 13% are literate. Also, the literacy gap between boys and girls aged 15 to 19 is only 11% [25]. Therefore, a 2007 UNESCO and UNICEF report addressed this issue of educating girls from a rights-based approach. Three interrelated rights were specified to handle the situation and must be addressed in concert to provide an opportunity for all.

Educated women better provide for their families.
(Image created in Piscart)

EDUCATION
A BASIC HUMAN RIGHT

Drawing from the quote of the president of the Ane Osiobe International Foundation, Dr. S. A. Osiobe, "I believe Education in Africa is a basic human right. No one should ever forgo education because of the cost." The following rights need to be enacted to realize the president's dream.

1. *The Right to Quality and Accessible Education:* Education must be available for, accessible to, and inclusive of all children, especially in the .com era. In the present day, the Internet has made education available to all. Many online schools are offering diverse courses and awarding certificates to students. With the advent of online training, there is no distance barrier to scholarship; learning is now localized. It is also interesting that some reputable institutions offer

free courses, thereby eliminating the cost of tuition. The various certifications are valid if they are verifiable and from recognized institutions. This levels the educational playing field for people who can't attend a conventional university. Female children who, for one reason or another, cannot leave home can still access quality education online as long as they have access to the Internet. The Internet also gives employment opportunities to women who desire to work from home; many corporations, far and near, now offer freelancing and localized work online. The networking opportunities online are enormous; people can now create groups and make friends across the globe.

2. *The Right to Respect within the Learning Environment* – People must have a level playing ground for active, effective, and efficient learning. The issues surrounding gender quality should be addressed within the education system. Education must be consistent with human rights, have equal respect for culture, religion, and language, and be free from violence [3] [25]. Girls' education in Nigeria has improved over the decades but is far from satisfactory [7]. However, there is room for improvement by using appropriate measures. Introducing laws that create a safe learning environment for everyone is an effective

way to start—at the same time, enforcing the consequences of breaking the rules, directly or indirectly.

Nigerian policymakers should see children's education as a serious issue to ensure a better future for the nation. Parents should be encouraged to send their daughters to school, and this can be done through awareness programs at all levels and communities. The provision of affordable or accessible education for children from poorer backgrounds should be encouraged, and this would promote the reduction of illiteracy in the nation [7].

A classroom awaiting both boys and girls.
(Image created in OpenArt)

Girls on the northern side of Nigeria face many socioeconomic and cultural barriers to education compared to those in the southern part of the country (World Bank, 2017). Due to higher-than-average poverty in the Northern region, cultural norms, religious practices, poor infrastructure, and Boko Haram violence. The World Bank has joined governments, NGOs, private sectors, individual donors, and multilateral organizations to advance a multi-sectoral approach to overcome these challenges facing the education crisis within the country. Some of these initiatives, fostered by the World Bank and NGOs around the world, include but are not limited to:

- Providing conditional cash transfers: The various sponsors of formal education have adopted a condition for sending financial assistance; this includes a fair balance of male-female gender among students to receive cash support.
- Providing stipends or scholarships: The World Bank and many other NGOs encourage female education by giving wages and fellowships to promising female students.
- Reducing the distance to school: annexing schools to rural areas will effectively remove the distance barrier to learning. Using an internet connection is also effective in bringing education closer to the female populace.

- Creating a safe space for a dialogue with boys and men on the female education issue: In cases of cultural and religious barriers to female education, the World Bank and other NGOs organize programs for open discussions and debate on female education for enlightenment.

- Establishing and enforcing equal employment laws at the federal level: The clamor for equal employment opportunities for both male and female sexes has been a significant activity of NGOs with support from the World Bank.

Assembly at Gwagwalada, Nigeria
Image © Ane Osiobe International Foundation

33

- Building safe and inclusive learning environments for children: It is essential that learning takes place in a safe and secure environment. Insecurity, in itself, is a barrier to education.

- Increasing the legal age for marriage to 18: Early marriage is a significant obstacle to female education. Efforts have been extended towards eradicating child marriage and the adoption of 18 years of age as the minimum marriage age for both sexes.

- Addressing violence against girls and women: The female populace stands to be most vulnerable to abuses and attacks from their male counterparts; it is crucial to address the issues of violence with stringent penalties against offenders. This is a step towards encouraging female education.

ACTIVITIES OF NON-PROFITS IN PROMOTING FEMALE EDUCATION WORLDWIDE

Many NGO activities have been channeled towards the education of girls around the world. Both government and non-governmental organizations have contributed significantly to this topic. The actions of NGOs include but are not limited to sensitization of communities regarding the need for female education and scholarship packages within and outside Nigeria.

The Female Art Foundation (GCAF) is a Nigerian NGO with the mission of "Providing a supportive environment that educates and inspires underserved girls in Africa using Arts" [26]. Over the years, the organization has engaged over 200,000 girls in its program, touching over 200 communities [26]. Their activities include making learning for every girl, organizing training classes, workshops, seminars, and other events, and investing effectively in girls to end child marriage. All activities of the foundation are tailored towards achieving SDG goal 4, which is to *"Ensure inclusive and equitable quality education and promote lifelong learning opportunities for all"* [26].

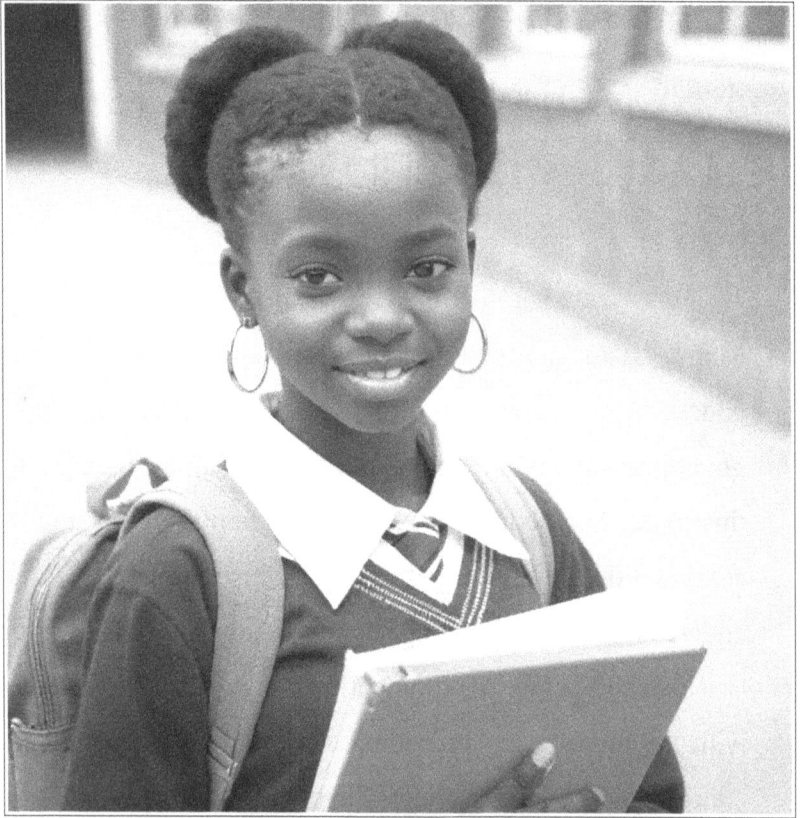

A young girl eager for school to start.
(Image created in OpenArt)

The Girl Power Initiative (GPI) is a Nigerian NGO formed in 1993 by Bene Madunagu and Grace Osakue. It commenced its activities in July 1994 in Cross River and Edo States. This NGO encourages female children to learn about the benefits of formal education. The organization was created to *'Promote the rights of children, especially girls, and mobilize them for development and participation through research, education, and action-oriented programs directed towards their empowerment"* [27]. The organization's activities are spread across Nigeria, creating awareness of children/youth education and trafficking. They organize community stakeholder meetings, establishing groups to strengthen girls and women's rights in national societies.

Student event at Lugbe, Nigera
Image © Ane Osiobe International Foundation

The Mother and Girl-Child Protection Initiative (MAGI): Alhaja Adijat Titilade Malik founded the foundation in 2012, a non-profit, non-religious, non-governmental organization committed to protecting mothers & girls. Its aim and objectives revolve around giving a future of freedom, dignity, and emancipation to women and girls who are less fortunate in communities through training, advocacy, and empowerment.

Student event at Lugbe, Nigera
Image © Ane Osiobe International Foundation

The Girl Child Concerns (GCC) is a non-governmental organization in Nigeria. They aim to improve the lives of young people, especially girls, through various interventions, which include but are not limited to improved educational opportunities and life skills development; ensuring the availability of broad-based education for all young people regardless of class or gender; the application of holistic interventions that meet the needs of vulnerable adolescent girls especially those from low-income rural areas, disadvantaged and underserved groups like married adolescent and girls in humanitarian settings [28].

The Girls Who Code is an NGO established by Reshma Saujani in 2010 when she observed the wide gap between male and female IT specialists. In 1995, about 37% of computer scientists were women; today, only 24% of them are female [29]. Since computer programming is the future for most professions, she believed that if practical steps are not taken, only 1 out of every five computer programmers will soon be female, which could lead to a high unemployment rate among women. To prevent this, the organization is working towards training female engineers in the United States and closing the gender gap in technology. Their platform provides learning opportunities, clear pathways, and supportive sisterhood of peers and role models. About a million girls have been served indirectly until now, and about 180,000 have been directly served.

Ejiro U. Osiobe

NOTABLE NIGERIAN WOMEN WHO SHAPED THE COUNTRY

Nana Asma'U

Known as the first Islamic Feminist of Nigeria, Nana Asma'U bint Shehu Usman dan Fodiyo is a poet, scholar, teacher, polymath, and intellectual. Her false stereotypes as a Muslim woman in history, as devalued, silenced, and subjected to domestic duties, led to the noble standard of the intellectual milieu in which the Sokoto society is known today. Asma'u translated the Quran into Fulfude, Hausa, and al-Jawzi's Sifaatu Safwa; she has over 60 published works that have survived and are being studied.

"Worldly greatness is not a worthy aim, but personal goodness—patience and generosity—is what makes a person pious."

Dr. Ngozi Okanjo Iweala

A renowned economist, scholar, and author with over ten honorary degrees, Dr. Ngozi Okonjo Iweala was born in the BIG heart of the country "Delta State." She is the first female and a two-time Federal Republic of Nigeria finance minister. She was named one of the 50 most outstanding leaders in 2015 by Fortune magazine and one of the world's 100 most influential people by Time magazine.

"I believe that when you find problems,
you should also find solutions."

Queen Amina

A scholar and warrior queen, Amina Mohamud, ruled in the mid-sixteenth century from Zazzau, Kaduna State, Nigeria. She was the first woman in Nigeria to become the Sarauniya (queen) in a male-dominated society. Named Magajiya (Heir Apparent), she commanded an army of 20,000-foot soldiers and 1000 cavalry troops.

"My legacy is defending my people,
and my wall will stand for generations."

Obiageli Ezekwesili

Obiageli Ezekwesili is one of the co-founders of the Transparency International Organization. Oby Ezekwesili is best known for her leadership of the Nigerian campaign to free the Chibok schoolgirls kidnapped by the Boko Haram group. She was once the minister of education of the Federal Republic of Nigeria and presently serves on the board of the World Wildlife Fund.

"Don't be voiceless when you have had the privilege of being educated."

Sarah Nnadzwa Jibril

Sarah Nnadzwa Jibril is a psychologist and politician. She was the first female presidential candidate of a major political party in Nigeria. Business Insider listed her among 17 powerful women who have shaped Nigerian culture.

"My aim is to bring the culture of ethics into Aso-Rock."

Margaret Ekpo

Margaret Ekpo is Nigeria's first feminist; Margret obtained a Diploma in Domestic Economics in 1948. With her skills and knowledge in the field, she established the first business incubator in the nation that groomed young girls in tailoring and home economics.

"At the time, it wasn't easy, but I made myself a promise to be educated at all cost."

Folorunsho Alakija

Folorunsho Alakija is a billionaire and Lagos native; Mrs. Alakija is best known for starting a successful fashion label called "Supreme Stitches" and the Rose of Sharon Foundation that helps widows and orphans through scholarship and business grants. Today, she is heavily involved in the Commonwealth Business Forum and is a prolific and inspirational writer.

"Do not allow people with a negative mindset to linger around you. If I can achieve Billion-dollar status, so can you."

Funmilayo Ransome-Kuti

Funmilayo Ransome-Kuti is an educator, political advocate, and women's rights activist; she was the first woman to attend a school in her community and to drive a car in the country. She established the Abeokuta Women's Union and the Abeokuta Ladies' Club. Chief Kuti fought hard for women's rights, representation in government offices, and fair taxes on farm & market women. After fighting tirelessly to further women's access to education and healthcare in Nigeria, she is a Lenin Peace Prize recipient.

"As for the ill charges against me, I'll pay them no mind because I'm beyond them, and history will remember me."

Ladi Dosi Kuwali

Ladi Dosi Kuwali is a born native of the Federal Capital Territory from the village of Kwali, Gwari region. She is a proud Potter, honored on the twenty naira note, and a pottery professor at Ahmadu Bello University (ABU). She was awarded an honorary doctorate from ABU. Zaria. Ladi Kuwali received the national honor of the Officer of the Order of the Niger, the Silver Award for Excellence, and the Tenth International Exhibition of Ceramic Art, Smithsonian Institute, Washington, DC, USA. In her honor, the Abuja Pottery was renamed the Ladi Kwali Pottery, and a significant street in Abuja is called Ladi Kwali Road.

"My pots will show Kwali to the world."

Dr. Dora Akunyili

Dora Nkem Akunyili, Ph.D., is a native of Anambra state, Nigeria. She was the director-general of the National Agency for Food and Drug Administration and Control (NAFDAC) for eight years. During administration, she created extensive awareness about drug counterfeiting and forced the countering industry to shut down. She has over 100 awards, including but not limited to the Time Magazine Award, the Order of the Federal Republic, and the Integrity Award.

"If we fail to act now on the war on fake drugs,
history will not forgive us."

Capt. Chinyere Onyenaucheya

Captain Chinyere Onyenaucheya Kalu is the first Nigerian female to fly a plane, captain a commercial aircraft, and lead the Nigerian College of Aviation Technology. She is a member of the Nigerian Women Achievers Hall of Fame and the Order of the Federal Republic of Nigeria.

"Let's fly, 9ja!!!"

Chioma Ajunma

Chioma Ajunma is an Olympian and law enforcer. She is the first African woman to win a gold medal in a field event. Chioma played for the Super Falcons during the Women's World Cup of 1991 and is an anti-doping activist in the sports industry.

"The spirit of Sportsmanship should not only be on the field."

Dr. Elizabeth Awoliyi Abimbola

Elizabeth Awoliyi Abimbola, M.D. is the first physician in Nigeria, the first West African woman to become a licensed royal surgeon, and the second to qualify as an orthodox-medicine-trained physician. Elizabeth has won the Order of the Federal Republic, served as the Child Care Voluntary Association president, and was a Business and Professional Women's Association member. She was the first president of the Parish Women Council of Holy Cross Cathedral, Lagos, and she is an active member of Lagos Colony Red Cross, the Motherless Babies Homes, and the Dr. Abimbola Awoliyi Memorial Hospital was built in her honor.

"Healthcare and loving your neighbor are the same thing."

Dr. Ameyo Stella Adaevoh

Dr. Stella was a Lead Consultant Physician and Endocrinologist in Lagos, Nigeria. She is known for her efforts in diagnosing and containing the spread of Ebola in 2014. The Dr. Ameyo Adadevoh Health Trust, an NGO, was created in her honor.

"For the greater public good,
I'll keep my Hippocratic Oath."

Amina J. Mohammed

A scholar and professor at Columbia University, Amina J. Mohammed is the 5th deputy secretary General of the United Nations. She founded the Afri-Project Consortium and the Center for Development Policy solution. Amina has chaired the Advisory Board of the United Nations Educational, Scientific and Cultural Organization (UNESCO) Global Monitoring Report on Education (GME). She has received the Order of the Federal Republic and was instrumental in bringing about the 2030 agenda for sustainable development.

"My journey has taught me that the only purpose of power is to serve with the courage of one's conviction that all people in the world have the rights that must be respected."

Stella Obasanjo

Born in Warri, Delta State, Mrs. Stella Obasanjo was an activist and the first lady of Nigeria from 1999 to her death. During Obasanjo's administration, She campaigned against Female Genital Mutilation and in the rebuilding of Nigeria. In 1999, she established a Child Care Trust Foundation for caring for disabled children in Nigeria and won the African Civic Responsibility Award.

"I believe in the Spirit of female activism."

CONCLUSION

The importance of educating women in our society cannot be overemphasized. This book discusses why the Nigerian community and other nations must invest in women and education. If we desire a better future, educating the female population is necessary. Looking at the achievements of the selected women in the book, there is no doubt that more can be achieved if women are given equal opportunities. The progress of any society is relative to the opportunity it offers women to help build it. To address the cultural justification of educating boys over girls is the same reason for every woman to access equal quality education in Nigeria.

The Ane Osiobe International Foundation was founded
in honor of Mrs. Ann Eloho Osiobe.

REFERENCES

[1] Leadership Report, "Why Girl-Child Education is Important," 21 7 2017. [Online]. Available: https://leadership.ng/2017/07/21/girl-child-education-important/. [Accessed 23 7 2019].

[2] E. U. Osiobe, "An Overview of Argentina's Educational Policies," The Ane Osiobe International Foundation, Abuja, 2021.

[3] E. U. Osiobe, " Protecting the Consumer: A Simplified Understanding of Antitrust Law," *American Journal of Law and Practices,* pp. 1-13, 2023.

[4] E. U. Osiobe, "Human Capital, Capital Stock Formation, and Economic Growth: A Panel Granger Causality Analysis," *Journal of Economics and Business,* vol. 3, no. 2, pp. 569-582, 2020.

[5] UNICEF, "Girls' Education; A Lifeline to Development," 2016. [Online]. Available: www.unicef.org: https://www.unicef.org/sowc96/ngirls.htm. [Accessed 22 7 2019].

[6] The World Bank, "Girls Education," 2017. [Online]. Available: https://www.worldbank.org/en/topic/girlseducation. [Accessed 23 7 2019].

[7] V. Falae, "Girl Child Education in Nigeria: Problems and Prospects," 7 2018. [Online]. Available: https://www.legit.ng/1124635-girl-child-education-nigeria-. [Accessed 23 7 2019].

[8] E. Ebunife, "Girl Child Education in Nigeria," 18 6 2018. [Online]. Available: https://infoguidenigeria.com/girl-child-education-nigeria/. [Accessed 24 7 2019].

[9] E. U. Osiobe, "An Overview of Bolivia's Educational Policies," The Ane Osiobe International Foundation, Abuja, 2021.

[10] E. U. Osiobe, "An Overview of Brazil's Educational Policies," The Ane Osiobe International Foundation, Abuja, 2021.

[11] E. U. Osiobe, "An Overview of Chile's Educational Policies," The Ane Osiobe International Foundation, Abuja, 2021.

[12] E. U. Osiobe, "An Overview of Colombia's Educational Policies," The Ane Osiobe International Foundation, Abuja, 2021.

[13] E. U. Osiobe, "An Overview of Costa Rica's Educational Policies," The Ane Osiobe International Foundation, Abuja, 2021.

[14] E. U. Osiobe, "An Overview of El Salvador's Educational Policies," The Ane Osiobe International Foundation, Abuja, 2021.

[15] E. U. Osiobe, "An Overview of Honduras' Educational Policies," The Ane Osiobe International Foundation, Abuja, 2021.

[16] E. U. Osiobe, "An Overview of Nicaragua's Educational Policies," The Ane Osiobe International Foundation, Abuja, 2021.

[17] E. U. Osiobe, "An Overview of Panama's Educational Policies," The Ane Osiobe International Foundation, Abuja, 2021.

[18] E. U. Osiobe, "An Overview of Peru's Educational Policies," The Ane Osiobe International Foundation, Abuja, 2021.

[19] E. U. Osiobe, Education in Latin America: Policies and Recommendations, Baldwin City: Imperium Publishing, 2023.

[20] E. U. Osiobe, "An Overview of Uruguay's Educational Policies," The Ane Osiobe International Foundation, Abuja, 2021.

[21] E. U. Osiobe, "An Overview of Venezuela's Educational Policies," The Ane Osiobe International Foundation, Abuja, 2021.

[22] E. U. Osiobe, "An Overview of the United Mexican States' Educational Policies," The Ane Osiobe International Foundation, Abuja, 2021.

[23] E. U. Osiobe, "A Literature Review and Overview of Performance Management: A Guide to the Field," *Sumerianz Journal of Business Management and Marketing*, pp. 2617-1724, 2020.

[24] A. R. Ronnlund, R. Hans and O. Rosling, Factfulness: Ten Reasons We're Wrong About the World – and Why Things Are Better Than You Think, Flatiron Books, 2018.

[25] E. Osiobe, "The National Economic Impact from Agriculture.," The Ane Osiobe International Foundation, 2018.

[26] GCAF, "Education," 2019. [Online]. Available: www.girlchildart.org: http://www.girlchildart.org/education/. [Accessed 30 7 2019].

[27] GPI, 2019. [Online]. Available: https://www.gpinigeria.org/about-us/. [Accessed 1 8 2019].

[28] GCC, "Girl Child Concerns," 2019. [Online]. Available: https://www.girlchildconcerns.org/#.

[29] Women Who Code, 2011. [Online]. Available: www.girlswhocode.com: https://girlswhocode.com/about-us/. [Accessed 7 4 2024].

Ejiro U. Osiobe

www.ingramcontent.com/pod-product-compliance
Lightning Source LLC
Chambersburg PA
CBHW071507210326
41597CB00018B/2698